Pea

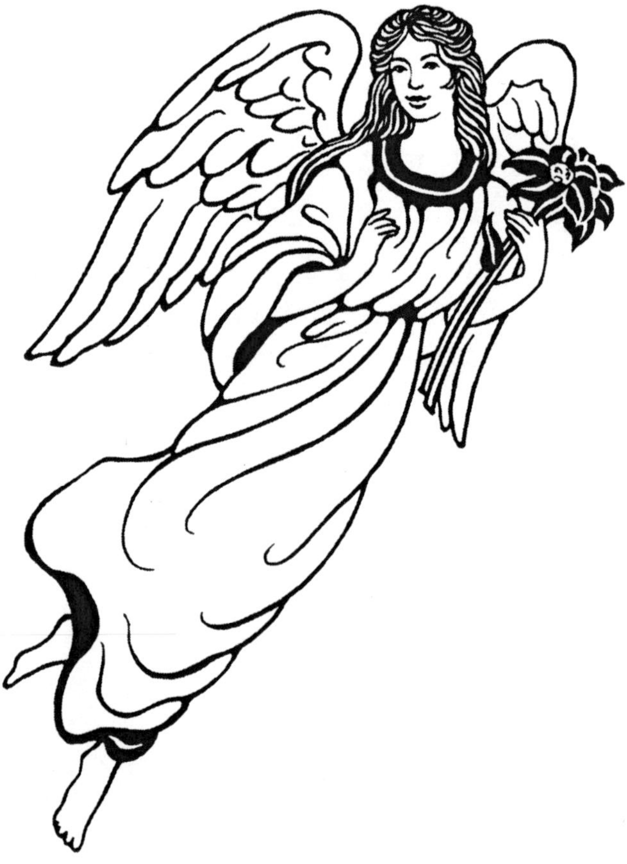

Peace, Be Still

Prayers and Affirmations

*Inspiration
for Family Caregivers*

Written by:
Rev. Gregory L. Johnson
Rev. Marion A. Gambardella

Compiled and Edited by Lisa Isom
Creative Director: C. Linda Dingler

BALBOA
PRESS
A DIVISION OF HAY HOUSE

Copyright © 2013 Rev. Gregory L. Johnson and Rev. Marion A. Gambardella

All rights reserved. No part of this book may be used or reproduced by any means, graphic, electronic, or mechanical, including photocopying, recording, taping or by any information storage retrieval system without the written permission of the publisher except in the case of brief quotations embodied in critical articles and reviews.

Balboa Press books may be ordered through booksellers or by contacting:

Balboa Press
A Division of Hay House
1663 Liberty Drive
Bloomington, IN 47403
www.balboapress.com
1-(877) 407-4847

Because of the dynamic nature of the Internet, any web addresses or links contained in this book may have changed since publication and may no longer be valid. The views expressed in this work are solely those of the author and do not necessarily reflect the views of the publisher, and the publisher hereby disclaims any responsibility for them.

The author of this book does not dispense medical advice or prescribe the use of any technique as a form of treatment for physical, emotional, or medical problems without the advice of a physician, either directly or indirectly. The intent of the author is only to offer information of a general nature to help you in your quest for emotional and spiritual well-being. In the event you use any of the information in this book for yourself, which is your constitutional right, the author and the publisher assume no responsibility for your actions.

Any people depicted in stock imagery provided by Thinkstock are models, and such images are being used for illustrative purposes only. Certain stock imagery © Thinkstock.

Cover image "Maria' by artist, Sasha Kinens, from the collection of Dana and Elisa Pionek. We express gratitude for being able to use.

Printed in the United States of America.

ISBN: 978-1-4525-6922-2 (sc)
ISBN: 978-1-4525-6924-6 (hc)
ISBN: 978-1-4525-6923-9 (e)

Library of Congress Control Number: 2013905297

Balboa Press rev. date: 4/29/2013

This book is dedicated to:

In Memoriam

Joseph Polacek
Giovanni Consiglio
Sarah Isom

And the millions of other care recipients blessed with the ultimate gift, the sacrifice made for another in their time of need.

"There is someone out there who needs me as much as I need them. Bring us together"

Contents

	Page
A Note Of Welcome	9
Foreword	15
Faith	19
Gratitude	21
Anger	23
Acceptance	26
Blessings	28
Comfort	30
Surrender	32
Belief	34
Forgiveness	36
Doubt	38
Fear	40
Healing	42
Renewal	44
Support	46
Strength	48
Celebration	50
Reflection	52
Understanding	54
Guidance	55

Honor	57
Thanksgiving	59
Power	61
Rest	63
Compassion	65
Release	67
Appreciation	69
Grace	71
Love	73
Wisdom	75
Peace	77
Family Caregiving Resources	79
Care for the Family Caregiver	88
10 Tips for Family Caregivers	90
Cuidados para el Cuidador de la Familia	91
10 Consejos para los Cuidadores de la Familia	93
Helpful Tips for Family Caregivers	97
Caregiver Health: Taking Care of Yourself	101

A Note Of Welcome

From
Reverends Johnson and Gambardella

WELCOME to the world of family caregiving. YOU ARE NOT ALONE. Both Marion and I have recently concluded the respective caregiving journeys for our life partners, hers, Giovanni, and mine, Joe, to whom this book is dedicated with love and gratitude.

None of us is ever trained in family caregiving and yet in the United States alone today there are 65.7 million of us, representing a donation of services valued (if we were paid in 2009 terms) of $450 U.S. billion. That is HUGE.

Family caregivers are the very backbone of the world's health care system.

A family caregiver can have many definitions but two of our favorites come from a noted expert and family caregiver, Carol Levine: A *"family caregiver is a person who shows up and stays to help"* . . . . .or a *"person who is always on call."* Sounds familiar, doesn't it?

In this introduction we want to share a few specific thoughts and then conclude with why—in addition to honoring the memory of our loved ones—we put together a wonderful team to write this book. *A few things all family caregivers must remember:*

We are dealing with CAREgiving, not CUREgiving. We suddenly in many cases realize that our loved one, relative, friend needs help and we are the person who is needed to provide it. It is very important that as we begin that we become aware of the condition AS IT IS; we accept this reality however difficult and then take action learning, sharing, exploring and caring.

FAMILY means many things. Family can be defined as FAMILY OF ORIGIN, our blood family; birth family. There is also a FAMILY OF CHOICE, persons with whom we have chosen to associate: a house of worship, a senior center, or even an apartment house. Many of us do not have members of our family origin either near us geographically or alive; we build supportive, loving relationships: families of choice.

There are many faces to caregiving. When one hears the words *family caregivers*, people naturally think of "grandma and grandpa." Indeed, caring for aging seniors has long been the hallmark and focus of caregiving. But there is more, there are:

- Grandparents raising grandchildren: THIS IS FAMILY CAREGIVING.
- People caring for loved ones with chronic conditions: THIS IS FAMILY CAREGIVING.
- People helping those experiencing end of life issues in the middle of life: THIS IS FAMILY CAREGIVING.
- Children helping to care for family and friends: THIS IS FAMILY CAREGIVING.

- Long distance caregivers: THIS IS FAMILY CAREGIVING.
- People tending to our Veterans whose wounds are sadly often chronic conditions and whose parents are now helping to raise their children: THIS IS FAMILY CAREGIVING.

Death is NOT always the final outcome to all caregiving journeys. Death is indeed part of life and it needs to be understood that death is NOT the failure of the medical system; it is part of life. In coming to terms with this, life becomes more wonderful.

Each of these scenarios is worthy of attention and a book in itself. Many fine resources are available. The appendix in the back of the book may help you get started, advance your present journey or explore new ideas, resources and tools.

THERE IS HELP.

The key is the need for family caregivers to identify themselves as FAMILY CAREGIVERS. Until we name our role, our task, our beliefs, our thoughts, we get defocused and rarely realize that *"Before I can care for you, I have to care for myself."* In truth you cannot give away what I do not have. If you are falling apart, you can do little to help another person.

As we clergy like to say: The Good Book says it in both halves, *"Love your neighbor AS yourself."* Not more than; less than; instead of . . . . . . .but AS YOURSELF. Thus, we need to care for ourselves: BODY . . . . .MIND . . . . .and SPIRIT.

This book has been written especially to assist you with a DAILY MOMENT FOR YOU AND YOUR GOD as you understand that name in this moment and time.

You do have a lifetime to come to understand that often misused name. Perhaps, you are one of many who have been wounded by someone else's concept of the Divine . . . . .again, you are not alone; but you do not need to remain in that state . . . . . . explore, question, dig, learn, and remember to take time to "Be still and know that I am God." . . . . . . .PEACE, Be Still.

On the other hand you may be a person steeped in faith and in a tradition that blesses you. Connect with that great source of love and strength.

Remember, we are all Children of God; and members of one race: the Human Race. Let us each remember, WHO WE ARE: *beloved children of God;* and that tells us WHOSE WE ARE: *we are God's own creation; brothers and sisters ALL.* Then we can ask WHAT DOES THAT MEAN: *a life of love and service.* FAMILY CAREGIVERS in action, in love, in service.

Now as you go forward, we invite you to do as we did and continue to do. Structure your caregiving so that at a specific time or times each day you take a few moments to read one Prayer, the Affirmation for living and the suggested Scripture.

If time allows, add other readings that help you to resonate with the Divine and allow strength, love, renewal, and comfort to fill your being that you can continue to CARE. As you go forward, know that you are in our prayers and we ask you to complete the circle and remember us.

PEACE, Be Still............With love,
Greg+ and Marion+

FAMILY CAREGIVERS
united in
LOVE and SERVICE, ALL

Foreword

This book was written to offer three, essential things to help caregivers in their time of service:

1. Prayers: When we pray we commune with God and feel God's presence within. Prayer is talking to God. We realize that God is greater than anything we may encounter and that God's power eliminates fear, uncertainty and unhappiness. Our faith in God gives us strength in spirit, mind and body.

2. Affirmations: An affirmation is a positive statement of faith. By affirming our Oneness with God and praying for inner strength, we experience a peace.

Always begin your affirmation with "This I believe" to strengthen your faith.

Always end your affirmation with "Thank you Father." The power of praise can bring about miracles.

3. Scripture: According to Reverend Thomas R. May Director: American Bible Society, if prayer is our talking to God, Scripture is where God talks to us. Countless millions of people throughout the centuries have found faith, hope and comfort in the message of the Hebrew and Christian Scriptures. You may want to consider these simple steps when approaching Scripture:

Find a quiet place to slowly read a passage.

Meditate on the passage, asking yourself what the text is saying to you

Pray, asking God how you should respond to the passage

Act, applying to your life what God's Spirit reveals through your reading and meditation.

Peace, Be Still

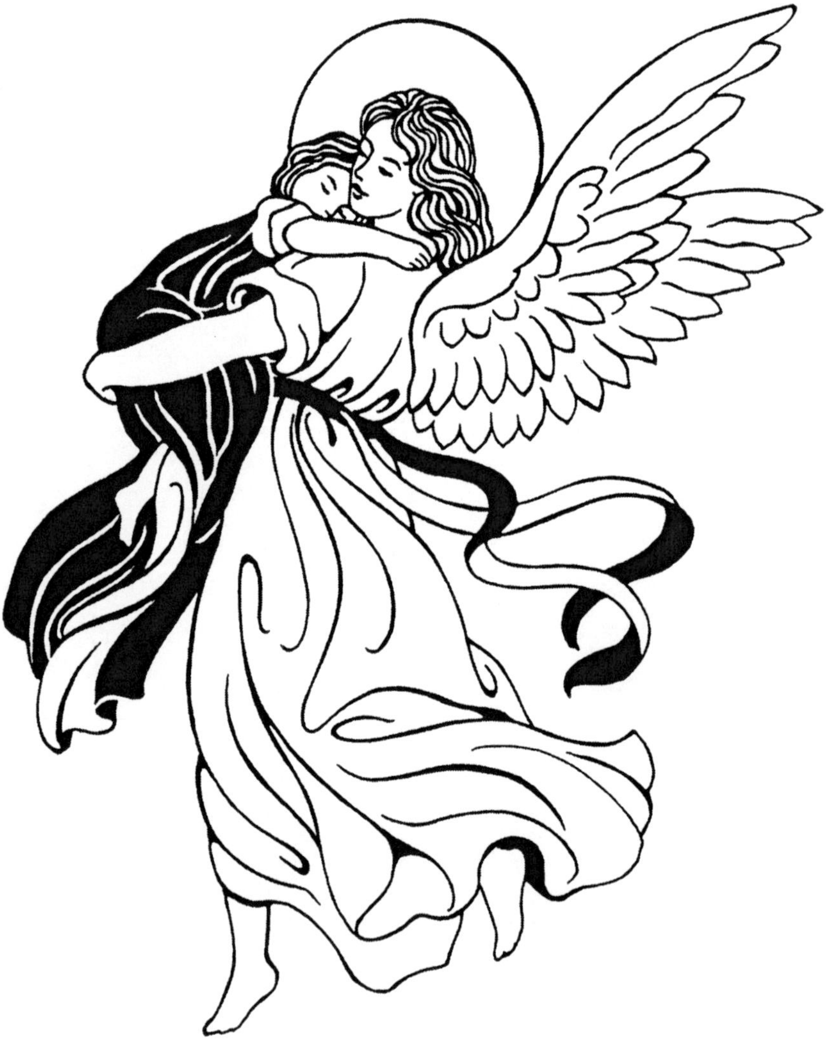

Faith

This is the day that the Lord has made. Let us rejoice and be glad in it.

This day is ours. Oh, Divine Spirit let this be our day for caring—for us and for others.

We have no idea what lies ahead. But with You, Father, there is goodness and light. We surrender this day, our loved ones and ourselves to your Divine and blessed care.

We know that all things are possible with You. The whole world is yours. In Divine Spirit we live and move and have our being and the greater world to come for eternity. In truth they are one, for You are one and we are one in You.

I go on my way in the strength of the Lord. And it is so.

Forever and ever, Amen

Today's Affirmations:
- Where there is doubt, I keep the faith.
- In God I trust.
- I am strong and secure in the love of God.
- Through the power of God in me, I now make a new start.

Hebrews 11:1

Now faith is the assurance of things hoped for, the conviction of things not seen.

Gratitude

Creator of each and every day, we greet this day with joyous expectation, knowing we are not alone. Thank You for this night of peace and quiet and for continuing life today. Thank You for each and every person we will meet this day, each is a brother and sister known or unknown to us, but all precious in your sight.

Yesterday is gone, tomorrow has not come. Keep us in this day and only in this day. You have promised to give us strength to meet each and every challenge.

We now claim that strength and go forward in joy and courage.

We are your children. You are our Father, our Mother and we trust in your loving protection and strength, now and forever.

And it is so.

TODAY'S AFFIRMATIONS:
- Each day I thank God for new opportunities.
- Dear Lord, I bless and appreciate this day.
- I recognize and give thanks for unlimited possibilities.
- I give thanks for each opportunity to create growth and achievement

Philippians 4:6

Do not worry about anything, but in everything by prayer and supplication with thanksgiving, let your requests be made known to God.

Anger

Today was truly not the success I has hoped for; everything seemed to overwhelm me. I responded again and again in ways that I did not want. I keep feeling angry. What was it? Why? How come?

As I pause and reflect, I come to God for guidance knowing that You have already forgiven me . . . Give me grace to do the same. For just a moment, that may be all I can muster. I sit quietly and take long, slow deep breaths, renewing my spirit and love. I begin to be calm and centered.

I begin to see the FEAR that is behind all my actions and reactions. Fear of being alone, fear of letting go, fear of accepting your will for it is very different, strange, new and unfamiliar. When fear comes, I burst out in anger expressed in many ways at others and myself. I respond in ways I do not want to act out.

Oh Father, Mother God . . . . Thank You for this reality of my humanity, my brokenness and my limitations. Heal me, strengthen me and bless each person against whom I have raged, reacted or behaved inappropriately. I truly am sorry. Help me to forgive myself. Help me to re-center myself in You and know your PEACE.

Help me to grow through this day, through this behavior and through this realization that it is FEAR that underlies so many of my emotions. This is not who

You created me to be. Help me to hear your words: BE NOT AFRAID . . . FOR I AM YOUR GOD AND WILL STRENGTHEN YOU! I know this is true . . . In rest, in peace, I give thanks for love, goodness and serenity. Oh source of all peace . . . In God, I trust.

Amen and Amen.

Today's Affirmations:
- I cease to give my thought to the memory of unpleasant experiences of the past and to cease worrying about my future and things that have not happened yet.
- Today is the only time to live and to enjoy all the blessings of God.
- I visualize my good manifesting now in the Present.
- I let go of old thoughts and conditions and let God direct my life.

Joshua 1–9

Be strong and courageous; do not be frightened or dismayed, for the Lord your God is with you wherever you go.

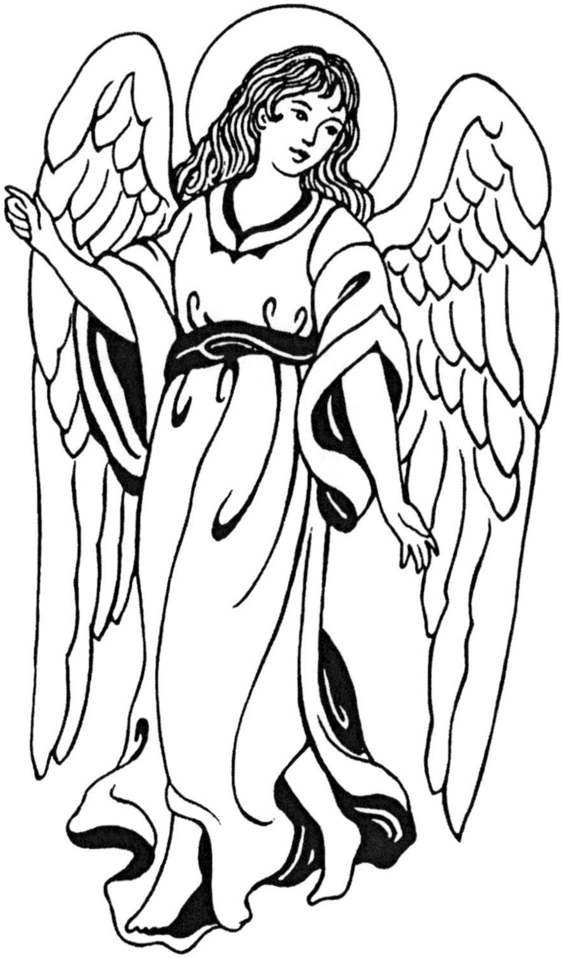

Acceptance

Which way do I turn? There are so many issues before me; I am overwhelmed and afraid. My loved one and I pray for strength, guidance, protection and wisdom to know the next right thing to do.

Keep us mindful that You are in charge. We are not. You are our Father, our Mother and we your children, no matter what our earthly age.

We surrender our fears, confusion, and our weakness to your almighty strength. We pause and hear your Word: "be still and know that I am GOD."

We are reminded that "In the beginning God" and not, "in the beginning me"

And in this truth we release, relax and are restored. And we give You thanks, now and forever more.

Amen

TODAY'S AFFIRMATIONS:
- I agree with God.
- Healing is taking place now.
- I allow the love of God to flow through me.
- All I need is already in me.

2 TIMOTHY 1:7

For God gave us a spirit not of fear but of power and love and self-control.

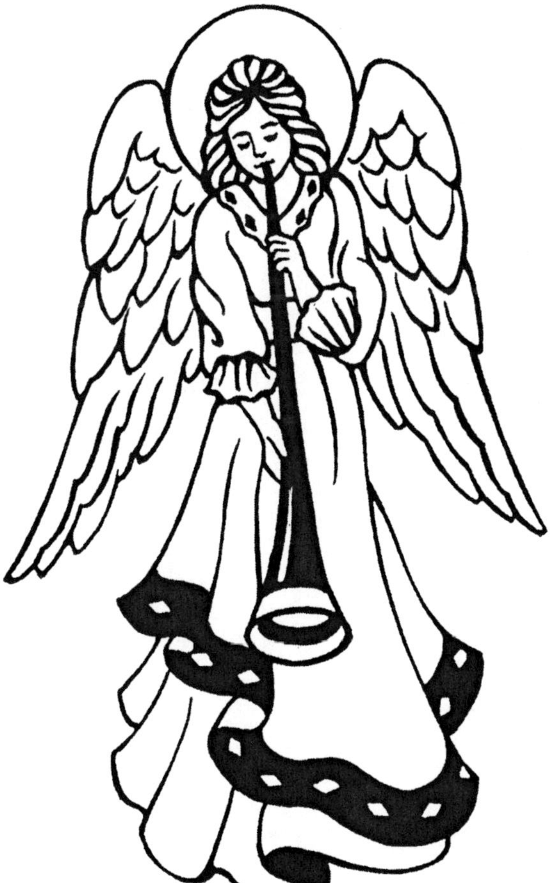

Blessings

Come Lord Jesus and be our guest and let these gifts to us be blessed...

Help us to hear and see this prayer as a daily affirmation of our co-creation and Divine partnership as we pray this prayer of invitation in all our affairs. Come Lord Jesus and be our guest in all we do, say, think and see. Let us practice the presence of the Divine in all we do. Oh Lord, come and be our guest.

And let all of life be gifts: the good and the seemingly difficult, for You are only good and You send only good. It is we who are locked in time and space, caught up in our earthliness, our humanity and our mortality.

Keep us mindful of our Divine nature, of our Oneness with You in whom we live and move and have our being.

Come Lord Jesus and be our guest. And let these gifts to us be blessed.

Amen

Today's Affirmations:
- The work of Spirit is done easily and perfectly through me.
- Each day I take time to listen to the still small voice within.
- I am a Wanted, Holy, Beloved Child of God.
- My life is full of promise.

Psalm 54:4

Behold, God is my helper; the Lord is the upholder of my life.

Comfort

Oh Lord, thank You for the promise that You will never leave me. No matter what is happening, no matter the difficulty, no matter the situation—You are there. Your love surrounds me and all for whom I care.

Underneath are the everlasting arms and into those precious arms I surrender myself and my loved one. Together with You we will walk forward. We will grow through each and every experience, knowing that You are with us through it all.

I will trust and not be afraid for You, Father God, Mother God, are ever near. All I need to do is close my eyes, take a deep breath and reconnect with the precious Gift of Life, the Breath of God with which I was born.

I now claim your Divine presence in my life, in every situation and circumstance and all is well, now and always.

Amen.

TODAY'S AFFIRMATIONS:
- Through the power of God in me, I am stronger than my fears.
- Whenever I feel afraid, I pray. I call a loving, accepting and trusting friend.

- The joy of God wells up within me.
- I am experiencing the comfort of God's presence in this moment.

Isaiah 41:10

Fear not, for I am with you; be not dismayed, for I am your God; I will strengthen you, I will help you, I will uphold you with my righteous right hand.

*S*urrender

Oh Divine Redeemer, give me grace to live in gratitude and surrender. I give thanks for every moment of my life. I thank You for each and every person with whom I have been blessed to walk through life. With some the walk has been long; with others it has been short. Each has been a blessing.

I thank You and I bless your Holy Name, precious Lord and Father.

When the time comes to let go, give me grace to let go with gratitude. Help me accept and to surrender my loved one to You, remembering that surrender is an act of love. It is in truth letting go to receive abundantly.

Oh Divine Friend, Eternal Partner . . . With You is life eternal and in You we are all one, now and always. Help me to live in the Eternal now. Heaven now right here on earth. Give me strength to live always in this joyous presence, practicing the presence of the Divine.

For in this there is no fear, no worry. There is only peace, joy and love.

I pray in your name. In you I live and move and have my being, one now and forever more with an attitude of gratitude and surrender.

Amen.

TODAY'S AFFIRMATIONS:
- I release self-doubt. I now surrender feelings of insecurity.
- I open my mind to Divine wisdom and all darkness is dispelled.
- I release all painful memories and allow healing to take place.
- God takes my hand and leads me safely through difficult times.

MATTHEW 11: 28

Come to me, all who are weary and heavy-laden, and I will give you rest.

Belief

Pray without ceasing and it is so. Pray until every waking moment is a moment of prayer in thought, word, and deed. In everything give thanks.

PUSH: Pray Until Something Happens. And it will.

Pray without ceasing until it brings peace and serenity. Pray until you are one with the Spirit of the Universe. God is ready to help. Pray without ceasing and let the thought of God be the balm for your fears, your worries and your pain. Pray without ceasing until you find healing for your hurts, your feelings and your emotional wounds.

Pray without ceasing until your doubts, fears and insecurities vanish as you affirm: God can and will solve this problem. And it is so . . .

And as you pray, let love, peace, joy, assurance, power, clarity and serenity flow within so that in turn, it may be given away. For as we receive, so do we give. With God we can have tolerance and joy to live and let live.

Pray without ceasing, giving thanks always.

Amen and Amen.

Today's Affirmations:
- On the wings of prayer, my soul soars above problems.
- God is the source of all my blessings. I am prospered.
- Today I allow the peace of God to reign in my mind and heart concerning my prayer request.

♦ Today I remind myself that God and I are in Divine partnership. My success is assured!

Mark 11:24

Therefore I tell you, whatever you ask in prayer, believe that you have received it, and it will be yours.

Forgiveness

Oh Father God, oh Mother God, I ask for your Divine help. I want to forgive and move on, but resentments, anger and perceived injustices will not leave me. There are times when I seem unable to rise above my own feelings.

Help me not to judge myself or others. Give me willingness to accept that I feel hurt, wounded and resentful.

I surrender each feeling, every resentment and each thought of anger and pain to You.

I am overwhelmed to feel your love. You do not judge my humanity and weakness. You make life perfect in my weakness. You make life holy and truly whole.

Give me wisdom to see my part in each issue, perhaps with the guidance of a trusted friend, a therapist, a clergy person. Teach me the lesson in my feelings that I may grow and be strengthened.

I now give thanks for these feelings. In each challenge I see You; I see your solution and your presence. I rejoice.

Now, I breathe in your love, your grace, your willingness and your peace.

I go on strengthened, renewed and blessed. Lord, make me a blessing to those who seemed a burden, a difficulty, a challenge. Grant this that I may witness your love always.

And it is so.

Today's Affirmations:
- Where there is hatred, I sow love.
- Where there is injury, I forgive.
- Where there is despair, I maintain hope.
- Where there is darkness, I radiate light.
- Where there is sadness, I cultivate joy.

Luke 6:37

Judge not, and you will not be judged; condemn not, and you will not be condemned; forgive, and you will be forgiven.

Doubt

Oh God of my understanding, help me. I am doing my best. But I am weak and human. Oh Divine Teacher, oh Divine Strength . . . Surround me, support me, and help me to be your hands, your eyes, your heart, your love in action. Help me not to waste time judging my success or failure. Help me just to act as if I know how to do this and I trust in You to produce the wisdom, action and the results.

We are, indeed, human beings locked in finite time and space. We are limited. You are eternal, unlimited and forever living. Help me to find that spark of Divine within me and to let it shine forth, not of my doing but of You, the Eternal Now.

Help me to grow one minute at a time, partnering with You and my sisters and brothers here on earth. There are people here and now who can help. They have been caregivers; they have expertise, experiences from which I can learn and find strength. Through them, I can hear your loving voice saying, "Be still and know that I am God. I love you and your care recipient"

Give me, oh God, the grace to hear your voice of peace, courage and strength. Give me the ability to hold the hand of my care recipient until at last I may place that hand into yours for all eternity.

"Oh blest communion, fellowship Divine. We feebly struggle; they in glory shine. Yet, all are one in Thee for all are thine. ALLELUIA."

Amen.

Today's Affirmations:
- God is greater than anything we may encounter; God's power within me helps eliminate fear.
- The miracle-working power of God is manifesting harmony, guidance, freedom, happiness, peace, prosperity and order in my life.
- God is life, health, perfect action, strength and vitality. I am created in the image and likeness of God.
- I have faith that God is responding to my every prayer.

Matthew 7:7–8

Ask and it will be given to you; search and you will find, knock, and the door will be opened for you. For everyone who asks receives and everyone who searches finds, and for everyone who knocks, the door will be opened.

Fear

Fear, at the root of so many of our other emotions, overwhelms and confounds. Is fear: Forget Everything And Run? Or is it: Face Everything And Recover? The choice is mine and yours.

Help me, Oh Father/Mother of us all, to choose the latter. Help me to understand when I am afraid, troubled by circumstances that are beyond me, powerless. Then, aware of my emotional state, let me accept it without judgment. I am human and fear is part of life and at this moment I am afraid. Let me accept this understanding that in awareness and acceptance I can move on to positive, bold, and love-filled action.

I cast out the fear in the name and power of the God of my present understanding or confusion. And so it is so.

Thank You for strength, for the peace that is now washing over me with abundance and assurance. And, I go on. I face everything and recover. I celebrate a life of co-partnership and co-creation; a life walking with my source of all peace, comfort, strength and joy.

Forever and ever. World without end.

Amen.

Today's Affirmations:
- I release feelings of fear. I give no power to thoughts of apprehension or worry.
- Regardless of appearances, I have faith in the power of God within to heal me on every level of my being.
- The guiding light of the Holy Spirit brightens my way.
- I allow true understanding to have dominion over feelings.

Psalm 27:1

The Lord is my light and my salvation, whom shall I fear?

Healing

Oh Father, Mother God, thank You for this reality of my humanity, my brokenness, my limitations. Heal me, strengthen me. Bless each person at whom I have raged, reacted, or behaved inappropriately. I am sorry. Help me to forgive myself. Help me re-center myself in You and know your peace.

I am exhausted and confused. Yet, when I reflect and rest, I know that I must care for myself before I can care for another. In caring for myself, I am preparing to better love and serve my care recipient—and others.

I pledge to "love my neighbor as myself." Today, tomorrow and always.

Oh source of every good and perfect gift, when I feel tired, afraid, overwhelmed, resentful or just out of sorts, please take me in your mighty arms and grant me willingness to surrender. Allow me to let go gently, to receive abundantly.

Lord, I surrender myself, my problems, my loved ones and my future into your hands and I trust in Thee. I remember with thanksgiving that You are infinite wisdom, infinite power, infinite strength. . . . and I claim with unwavering faith these resources for myself.

Help me to let go. Help me to let You, God, take charge.

TODAY'S AFFIRMATIONS:
- I am free. I am unlimited. There are no chains that bind me.
- I am master of my thoughts, feelings and actions.
- I am unhurried and unworried. I am at peace.
- I let go and let God manifest in my life as new adventure, unexpected pleasures and unlimited potential.

JEREMIAH 17:14

Heal me, O LORD, and I shall be healed; save me, and I shall be saved, for You are my praise.

Renewal

Oh Lord, thank You. When the pressures, the fears, the distractions of this worldly, material life become too much for me, I can stop, take a few very focused breaths, claim my spiritual being and begin my day all over in partnership with You, oh precious and ever-present God.

I hear You call, "Be still and know that I am God!" I need to hear that message again and again: "Be still and know that I am God."

Yes, You are God and every time I forget, I get into such difficulties physically, emotionally and spiritually. Thus, at this very moment with joy, gratitude, and happiness I begin my day anew.

Amen and Amen.

TODAY'S AFFIRMATIONS:
- I give thanks for each opportunity to create growth and achievement.
- I allow the spirit of God to nurture my inner self.
- I have all the wealth of the universe available to me.
- The power of God is at work in me and through me.

Romans 12:2

Do not be conformed to this world, but be transformed by the renewal of your mind, that by testing you may discern what is the will of God, what is good and acceptable and perfect.

Support

"Oh Lord, support us all the day long, until the shadows lengthen, and the evening comes, and the busy world is hushed, and the fever of life is over, and our work is done. Then in your mercy grant us a safe lodging, and a holy rest, and peace at last . . ."

This precious prayer has blessed my life so many times. As you stand not knowing where to turn as a caregiver, find rest in this prayer and strength for the changes that so often follow that point of culminated frustration. Know, that point wherein a radical change occurs.

Thank You, precious Lord, for such special prayers into which the circumstances of life breathe new meaning and greater understanding. Help us to treasure and to share with others the joy, the peace and comfort that certain prayers have given us. May we bless as we too have been blessed

In your Holy Name, Precious Lord take my hand.
Amen.

Today's Affirmations:
- Blessed are my hands, for they are the hands of God.
- Blessed is my heart, for it beats with the love of God.
- Blessed is my mind, for it is filled with the intelligence of God.
- The Spirit of Christ abides in me. I am whole, perfect and free.

1 John 3:17–18

If anyone has material possessions and sees a brother or sister in need but has no pity on them, how can the love of God be in that person? Dear children, let us not love with words or speech but with actions and in truth.

*S*trength

Oh Lord, thank You for the challenges of the past, for difficulties—physical, emotional, and spiritual. Thank You for walking me through what I never believed I could manage or do. In each I have learned of your love and your presence.

Each has taught me that in all things God can and will resolve the problem. It is not for me to find the details of the resolution. It is for me to seek the willingness to turn to You. And in turning to You, I learn even more of your power, your love, your wisdom and your presence. I am not alone.

May each step along this path point me more and more to You. May I ever learn and live knowing You dwell within my heart. I rejoice to affirm that I am not a human being trying to have a spiritual experience; I am a spiritual being, having a human experience.

It is then that I run to my true self, my spiritual self. I rest, knowing that with You all things are possible for me, for my care recipient, for my family and for the world.

I thank You for this day, for the present challenges and for the understanding that You, God, are setting all things according to your will.

You are providing all I need to live a life that is joyous, free, of service and of honor to You. And it is so.
Amen and Amen.

Today's Affirmations:
- I pray affirming that God's all-powerful and loving spirit is my constant support.
- True courage lives in me.
- I am confident and competent.
- God is on my side.

Deuteronomy 31:6

Be strong and courageous. Do not be afraid or terrified because of them, for the *Lord your God goes with you; he will never leave you or forsake you.*

*C*elebration

In everything give thanks.

Oh Lord, as a family caregiver I pray for the willingness and wisdom to celebrate You in everything and to keep celebrating the small victories, not just the big ones.

Let my care recipient and me rejoice in the small successes and in them find peace, joy and unity. Let us celebrate each seemingly small accomplishment, larger because of the challenges overcome in doing them. Let us celebrate these steps to wellness and positive caring, one step at a time.

We are climbing the mountain of wellness, health and wholeness. We are blessed to do it together, as caregiver and care recipient and most importantly as spiritual beings being partnered and sustained by You, our Divine source of all good—our eternal home.

And it is so. We celebrate.

Amen and Amen.

Today's Affirmations:
- I move through this day with a light and happy heart.
- Dear Lord, I enjoy this day! My expectations are good.
- Nothing can stand in the way of the good God has for me.
- Through God's grace, I live a life of love, faith and peace.

Romans 15:13

May the God of hope fill you with all joy and peace in believing, so that by the power of the Holy Spirit you may abound in hope.

Reflection

"You shall love your neighbor as yourself." Oh source of wisdom and strength and love... Help me to remember this as I go about my life as a family caregiver.

We call You by so many names... We are each on life's journey, struggling to make sense of so many challenges and circumstances. Sometimes I am totally exhausted and confused. Yet, when I stop, reflect and rest... I am aware that in order to go on, to serve, to help, to care...

I must care for myself, before I can care for another. In doing this, I am living this commandment in a way that I may not have understood it before. In caring for myself, I am preparing myself to better love and serve my care recipient and others: my neighbors, each of us YOUR children for eternity.

Help me to salute the Divinity within me, as I salute the Divinity in others, as I silently or loudly proclaim: **Namesté**... **Namesté**... The Divinity in me salutes the Divinity in You, my brothers and sisters of the world, of our Creator... and I see the good.

I see the Divine and I am ready to move forward again, strengthened in love, wisdom, patience, tolerance, understanding and acceptance.

I pledge to love my neighbor as myself, today, tomorrow and always.

Amen and Amen.

TODAY'S AFFIRMATIONS:
- I am a responsible person—toward others and toward myself.
- I want to honor my responsibilities as a caregiver. Yet I am also committed to myself.—I accept responsibility for my own health and well-being, as I do for my loved one.
- I am not discouraged or frustrated. I am willing to bless others and I am also willing, to bless myself.
- As I now recognize the Divinity in me, I recognize and affirm the Divinity in others and I am free to love fully.

PSALMS 51:12

Restore to me the joy of your salvation, and sustain in me a willing spirit

Understanding

No GOD; No PEACE. KNOW GOD; KNOW PEACE

Every day I seek to know You, most precious Friend, Father, God. Each day I am blessed to know more of your power, your strength, your love and, most of all, your presence.

Often I feel isolated, alone, left talking not to the loved one I knew, but to a disease I do not understand and often fear. It is then that I go within. I go to You, my Rock and my Redeemer. I find peace to carry on.

Thank You, Lord.

May my care recipient also know the power in: No GOD; No PEACE. KNOW GOD; KNOW PEACE

TODAY'S AFFIRMATIONS:
- God is the all-knowing, guiding presence that provides for me, no matter what the need.
- Even in the most challenging, difficult times, I affirm that I am never alone.
- God's gentle, loving presence is always within me, surrounding me, uplifting me, strengthening me.
- God is here and all is well.

JOHN 14:27

Peace I leave with You; my peace I give you. I do not give to you as the world gives. Do not let your hearts be troubled and do not be afraid.

Guidance

God is with me . . . Come into my heart today and every day. Fill me with your loving presence, with your strength and with your love. Help me amid the heat of summer, the rains of spring or the cold of fall and winter to know that You are born anew.

Amid the burdens and tasks of family caregiving, give me the wisdom to know that I can begin the day over at any time and recreate the season that helps me. Help me to know that when it all seems so wrong, so messed up, so confused and overwhelming, I can stop. I can decide for myself to begin again.

Help me as I begin my day again, to do so by seeing the spark of the Divine within me and within my care recipient being lit anew. Quietly let that light radiate throughout my being as I watch it radiate anew within my loved one for whom I am caring. May the light in me unite with the light within my loved one and may we be at peace, renewed and refreshed by your power and goodness.

God with us—yesterday, today and forever the same.

I am blessed, grateful, at peace and One with all Eternity. One with You, Father-Mother God.

Amen and Amen.

TODAY'S AFFIRMATIONS:
- Guided by God's light, I confidently move forward to greater fulfillment.
- I pray affirmatively with an expectation of unlimited blessings.
- I turn within and let God guide and direct me in all my ways.
- I look to God within me for guidance, courage and wisdom.

PSALM 18:32

It is God who arms me with strength and makes my way perfect.

Honor

The heavens are telling the glory of God. We are surrounded by your majesty and goodness. Oh Lord, thank You for the love which created us, the earth and the heavens.

We are surrounded by so many miracles; we are indeed miracles ourselves.

As we care for our loved ones, our care recipients keep us mindful that each of us is known to You. Each of us is precious in your sight. Each of us is a temporal gift one to the other. None of us knows how long we will be together. Teach us to treasure each and every moment we have—the good ones and the challenging ones.

Keep us mindful that our duty in life is to row. You will guide and navigate the seas of life. If, however, we decide to be the guide, director, navigator we need to remember that You do not row!

Keep us vigilant, humble, responsible, and loyal in love and service. Remind us to walk and grow through this life with our heads in the heavens with You and our feet here on earth, where our work remains.

And we give You thanks and praise today, tomorrow and forever . . . world without end.

Amen and Amen.

Today's Affirmations:
- I honor all paths to God.
- God is greater than anything we may encounter; God's power within helps eliminate fear.
- The miracle-working power of God is manifesting harmony, guidance, freedom, happiness, peace, prosperity and order in my life.
- I thank God for working in and through me at all times, guiding and supporting me in all ways.

Deuteronomy 6:5

You shall love the LORD your God with all your heart and with all your soul and with all your might.

Thanksgiving

Thank You for this day with all its successes and with all of its challenges. Today I may not be physically able to see a sunset, but I know it is there . . . and I am blessed. I am grateful. I feel your presence.

Sunrise, sunset, sunrise, sunset . . . I hear this song and it reminds me of your constant presence, your constant love, your constant support. It reminds me that You are ever present. And while I rest, You are caring, blessing, resolving and opening new doors in my life—new doors of possibility and of service.

Whatever the challenge was today, I surrender it to You, Oh God, as I seek to rest. I pray that I have met the challenges of today with grace and favor. Forgive that which I have done that I truly did not want to do. And give me grace to learn from each mistake and error.

As I prepare to rest, I surrender myself, my problems, my loved one for whom I am caring and my future into your hands. May your will be done forever.

Thank You for your love, always, Oh Lord. I thank You especially for my care recipient. I pray for healing, love, understanding and willingness in all matters we face together.

And God, grant me the serenity to accept the things I cannot change; courage to change the things I can; and wisdom to know the difference.

May your will, not mine, be done.

TODAY'S AFFIRMATIONS:
- God's power within me transcends all appearances.
- I see beyond the complexity of life.
- Any feelings of insecurity and confusion disappear in moments of prayer as I focus my thoughts on God.
- Recognizing the power of God beneath every facet of existence, I learn to "keep it simple." in my awareness.
- Whatever the appearance may be, God is simply all that I need.

PSALM 116:6

The Lord protects the simple; when I was brought low, he saved me

Power

Oh Divine friend, creator and sustainer of life, thank You for this promise and blessing of support, strength and constant presence. At times the burdens and challenges of my caregiving duties seem to be too much, too overwhelming, truly impossible. But with You, Oh God, all things are possible.

I picture a mountain tall, solid and majestic. I see in nature a live portrait of You, my rock and my redeemer. I breathe in your loving presence and power. I release my fears, and I am renewed.

I remember, FEAR means: Face Everything And Recover.

I give thanks, and then move on. I do not dwell on the negative, the fear-filled ideas. I acknowledge it and release it to You. I turn my thoughts to You. I rejoice that for me and for my care recipient, we claim in faith: "The Lord is my Shepherd, I shall not want."

And it is so.

Amen and Amen.

TODAY'S AFFIRMATIONS:
- I delight in the beauty and harmony of God's world.
- I choose to spend this day in perfect peace.
- I allow the Spirit of God to nurture my inner self.
- I rejoice in a life of discovery and participation.

Psalm 121:1

I will lift up mine eyes unto the hills, from whence cometh my help.

Rest

Be still and know that I am God. I am with You. I love You and will never let You go, for I am not in things outside, I am within You. Your own Divinity, your own piece of Heaven and Eternity, now and always.

Oh Divine friend, creator, redeemer and sustainer. How blessed to claim my Spiritual Inheritance. Awaken in me the willingness to accept your presence within and to grow more and more like You each day. In eternal Oneness with You, oh Father/Mother God.

I feel totally overwhelmed. I am lost, afraid, confused, panicked and alone—but I am not. YOU are with me. Keep me mindful that I am not God, You are. Together we can do all that is possible here on earth and in eternity for my loved one.

Help me to surrender my need to control and cure. I know that I cannot do these things. Help me to focus on caring, accepting the situation just as it is and being present in love—walking with another wherever that journey may lead.

Keep me focused on today, not yesterday with its regrets and errors, nor tomorrow which may never come at all. Keep me in today with all its challenges and blessings.

Keep me ever mindful of your presence in all persons, places, things and situations. In each, I claim your Spirit of love, goodness and peace. And in that, in YOU, I rest in peace. I know that I can begin this day again and again, returning in this prayer or another to You in whom I live and move and have my being. This I claim for myself and my loved one. And it is so.

Amen and Amen.

TODAY'S AFFIRMATIONS:
- I release the past and move forward with love in my heart.
- I am now tranquil as I experience love and peace within me.
- I lovingly take care of my mind, body and emotions. All is well in my life.
- The past has no power over me. I release all resentment that is holding me back.

2 CHRONICLES 14:7

We have sought the LORD our God. We have sought Him, and He has given us peace on every side.

Compassion

Grant us through this truth to live compassionate lives: caring, forgiving, understanding, empowering, respecting, accepting and loving all as we wish to be loved as well. In the words of St. Francis:

Lord, make me an instrument of your peace. Where there is hatred, let me sow love; where there is injury, pardon; where there is doubt, faith; where there is despair, hope; where there is darkness, light; and where there is sadness, joy.

O Divine Master, grant that I may not so much seek to be consoled as to console; to be understood as to understand; to be loved as to love. For it is in giving that we receive; it is in pardoning that we are pardoned; and it is in dying that we are born to eternal life. Amen

Lord, as family caregivers, we dedicate our lives anew to love and service. Strengthened and empowered by You, all powerful, all knowing, all caring and all loving.

Amen and Amen.

TODAY'S AFFIRMATIONS:
- I will allow true understanding to have dominion over feelings.
- My eyes behold peace. My lips speak peace. My feet walk in paths of peace.

- I give for the pure joy of giving.
- I have an endless capacity for love.

Ephesians 4:32

Be kind to one another, tenderhearted, forgiving one another, as God in Christ forgave you.

Release

Forgiveness frees, liberates and opens doors of possibilities. Help me to understand forgiveness, for in forgiving I reconnect with You—the great Forgiver of all.

Help me to look at situations and find my part in it. Help me to forgive myself, to own my part, to release my part and to release all related to the situation. Let me take action needed based on prayer or as suggested by a trusted counselor, sponsor, teacher, spiritual director or clergy advisor.

Peace will come.

Help me know that forgiveness does not necessarily mean fraternization. I can bless and move on. If my care recipient happens to be the center of my issue, I can offer prayer for them, as I pray for myself. And if an amend is needed, I can through loving service. make that amend to them as to myself.

Invite love to heal, triumph and bless without a word spoken, for that may be humanly impossible due to conditions beyond the present reality and condition. Let love transcend the physical and emotional limitations we now feel.

I reflect, I release, I let go.
And it is so.

Today's Affirmations:
- I bless, forgive and release the past.
- I am at peace with the God of my understanding.
- I let go, confident in the good that God provides.
- I choose forgiveness, and I am free.

Colossians 3:13

Bearing with one another and, if one has a complaint against another, forgiving each other; as the Lord has forgiven you, so you also must forgive.

Appreciation

Oh all powerful, almighty, all knowing and all loving God. I come to You with gratitude and joy. Thank You for this day and for my care recipient. Thank You for the strength to serve and to care.

I pray this day for all of us involved in family caregiving. At times it is overwhelming, frightening; but that is only when I forget You, Oh Lord. When I pause, breathe deeply and center myself in your everlasting love, I am at peace knowing that You can and will solve every difficulty, circumstance and issue.

Walk with me and all family caregivers, this day and every day. Help me to feel your Divine presence always with me and in me: Mind, Body, and Spirit.

Bless all professional caregivers, the doctors, nurses, aids, and all who work in health care. Bless their hands, eyes, hearts and minds in each and every task through which they are called to serve. Help me to help them have the clarity and understanding of my role as a family caregiver.

Let us serve in unity and harmony those whom You have given us to serve of love and care.

Amen and Amen

Today's Affirmations:
- I spend each day in appreciation of God's infinite love, freely given and gratefully received.
- As I go about this day, I bless all who cross my path.
- Today I take the first step of a new beginning.
- I am One with the harmonizing love of God.

Philippians 4:13

I can do all things through him who strengthens me.

Grace

Another week, another day, another hour, another minute with your grace, I made it. Thank You. I have made it safe thus far and I give thanks. I thank You for:

Good Orderly Direction that has come to pass.

Gratitude Overcoming Despair that is now mine.

Grace Overcoming Difficulties; there have been many on my caregiving journey.

For all these and in all these I see You, the Divine source of life. I give thanks.

Help me to remember that before I can care for anyone else I must care for myself. I know this is not selfish, it is totally necessary. Give me courage to act accordingly and to take time for me. Help me remember that self-care can be as simple as taking ten long, slow deep breaths or a simple walk around the block. Allow time for me to refresh, to relax, to renew and to revive myself for the tasks ahead and to partner with You the Divine Physician and Healer.

Help me to remember that by grace, I can be your hands, your eyes, your ears, and your voice to another. I am your child, your agent of love, your messenger of hope. I am powerless over the outcome or the present condition. I can only walk with my loved one as we both grow throughout the present reality and circumstance. I am not responsible for the outcome. I am only present for the present moment.

In faith I surrender my loved one and myself to your care. I trust in You to be our Rock, our Redeemer and our Friend for all eternity. And I give You the praise now and forever more. Amen and Amen.

Today's Affirmations:
- I am a child of God, receptive to good in every area of my life. I claim that good now.
- The light of God fills my heart and mind now.
- One with God, I am confident, wise and strong.
- The Grace of God blesses me abundantly.

Romans 8:28

And we know that in all things God works for the good of those who love Him, who have been called according to His purpose.

Love

What a precious picture, what a blessed truth . . . All around us are those we love here on earth now, those who have gone before us and those on that next plane of life beyond mortal sight and sound. Yet in Spirit we are ONE forever.

Help us draw upon their strength when we feel overwhelmed, used, abused, mistreated and depressed. Let their spirits surround us, motivate us, bless us and revive us once again.

Together we are marching through this early life, helping, loving and caring for one another. Striving to do unto others as we would have them do unto us. Let us be the hands, the ears, the arms, the heart, the smile, and the hugs of the Devine.

Giving love, joy and service one to another, until that blessed day when instead of living on earth knowing that God is with us here, we shall be with God in eternity. Forever we are blessed and with the blessed of all time.

Amen and Amen.

TODAY'S AFFIRMATIONS:
- I fill my mind with thoughts of love, service and joyous expectation.
- I am always ready to be loving, forgiving and understanding.

- No matter what challenges I am experiencing in the outer world, I know God's gentle, loving presence within me is comforting me, loving me and healing me and all is well.
- Drawing from an inner reservoir of God's love, I express love and harmony in all my relationships.

1 Corinthians 16:14

Let all that you do be done in love.

Wisdom

It is our journey here, a spiritual one, to become more like You, oh Father, Mother God. Like Jesus, our Master, Teacher, Way-Shower and Friend, we strive each day to increase our awareness of the presence of the Divine, to know your presence within us and to live in and to that glory.

You who are all knowing, all powerful, all loving and all caring. Teach me as I care for those You have given me to care for, to show love, patience, endurance, and strength. Help me to see You in even the most difficult of persons. Pain, anger, fear may greatly mask the Divine in my care recipient. But let my soul speak to soul, through prayer and loving actions.

Keep me ever mindful not to talk to sickness, but only to the soul, the Divinity within each person and myself.

Each and every day, change my heart. Oh God, make me more like You.

Amen and Amen.

TODAY'S AFFIRMATIONS:
- My emotions and actions are being guided by a blessed peace I know deep within me and I am reassured and comforted through each and every circumstance.
- Divine Wisdom leads me to my highest good.

- I thank God for blessings that pour forth abundantly in my life.
- With faith in the infinite wisdom of God within me, I move forward with clarity and assurance.

Acts 17:24, 27–28

The God who made the world and everything in it . . . Does not live in shrines made by human hands . . . Indeed he is not far from each one of us. For in Him we live and move and have our being.

Peace

Oh Caregiver of the World . . . I come before You today realizing that the only person on Earth I will spend my entire life with is me. My life—given and sustained by God—is a gift.

Help me to celebrate that You, my Divine source, are with me and together, we can travel the journey given to me, in love and service. Walking with You through this life reminds me of my Spiritual essence, my treasured spirituality.

With others I will be blessed to walk a portion of their life and mine.

I know I must let go of many of earthly loved ones, my family of origin, and my families of choice. I do so with surrender and gratitude. Surrender, for the reality is that their time is ended. Their life's work on earth is ended, they are at peace.

I am grateful for all we have shared, for memories that never leave, for lessons learned and embraced, and for love shared. I am grateful for the challenges which we did not bear in this life, for pain spared, for suffering not experienced.

Now, source of love and life . . . Give me strength and courage to go on and to remember and celebrate the past, but not dwell in it. Help me to go on with my journey, enriched, blessed and informed by my time with my precious loved one.

Lord, I surrender my loved one to You for all eternity, knowing that in You we are all one. I give thanks for the promise that, "Love bears all things, believes all things, hopes all things, endures all things. Love never ends."

In your Holy Name, Amen.

TODAY'S AFFIRMATIONS:
- When we surrender our little human self, we become one with our spiritual self.
- I accept joy. The light of God fills my heart and mind right now.
- I am loved. I am love. I am free.
- The peace and love of God radiates throughout my being.

1 CHRONICLES 16:11

Look to the Lord and his strength; seek his face always.

Family Caregiving Resources

The Alzheimer's Association
225 N. Michigan Ave., Fl. 17
Chicago, IL 60601-7633
312-335-8700
www.alz.org

The Association offers a range of resources; including a 24/7 help line, caregiver notebook, information on dementia, respite care, daily care, a caregiver stress check and more.

The ARCH National Respite Network and Resource Center
www.archrespite.org

The ARCH includes a **National Respite Locator**—an interactive tool to help caregivers locate respite services in their community—on its Web site. A respite service provides temporary care to children or adults with disabilities, or chronic or terminal illnesses.

Care for the Family Caregiver Initiative
EmblemHealth
55 Water Street
New York, NY 10041
646-447-6285
www.emblemhealth.com/familycaregivers

EmblemHealth's Care for the Family Caregiver (CFFCG) is a decade old initiative that offers a range of options to assist EmblemHealth employees and the community at large. Among other things, caregivers can take advantage of resources including Community outreach programs, print publications, including *Care for the Family Caregiver: A Place to Start,* produced in partnership with the National Alliance for Caregiving and published for the 2005 White House Conference on Aging, and social media sites.

The Centers for Medicare & Medicaid Services
7500 Security Boulevard
Baltimore MD 21244–1850
1–800-MEDICARE
www.medicare.gov

The Centers for Medicare & Medicaid Services, a branch of the U.S. **Department of Health and Human Services**, offers caregiver support and resources on its Web site.

Visit for information on caregiving topics, condition-specific resources, financial and legal support options, a discussion board and more.

DOROT
171 West 85th Street
New York, NY 10024
212-769-2850
www.dorotusa.org
E-mail: info@dorotusa.org

Among other things, this resource provides support groups, workshops and classes. There is a very nominal registration fee for Caregivers' Connections, an educational and support network for family caregivers, and participation in certain programs.

The Department of Health and Human Services—Administration on the Aging (AOA)
One Massachusetts Avenue NW
Washington, DC 20001
202-619-0724

www.aoa.gov

The AOA offers a robust collection of information for older adults, caregivers and professionals. The AOA Web site includes a tool that allows users to **get information on state agencies on the aging and available local resources.**

Faith in Action
Wake Forest University School of Medicine
Medical Center Boulevard
Winston-Salem, NC 27157
877-324-8411
www.fiavolunteers.org
E-mail: **info@fiavolunteers.org**

Faith in Action—The Robert Wood Johnson Foundation's interfaith volunteer caregiving program—makes grants to support volunteer, multi-faith local groups that come together and care for their neighbors with long-term health needs.

Family Caregiver Alliance
785 Market Street, Suite 750
San Francisco, CA 94103
415-434.3388 or 800-445.8106

Family Caregiver offers programs at national, state and local levels to support and sustain caregivers.

Family Caregiving 101
http://www.familycaregiving101.org/

New family caregivers will appreciate the information on this site. There is plenty to learn and read, like the *Top 10 Questions for Caregivers; Caring to Help Others: A Training Manual for Preparing Volunteers to Assist Caregivers of Older Adults*; and an extensive resource list.

Friends in Deed
594 Broadway, Suite 706
New York, NY 10012
212-925-2009
www.friendsindeed.org

Friends in Deed offers large facilitated groups focused on HIV, cancer, caregiving, grief and bereavement as well as one-on-one services, yoga and meditation classes, and workshops/seminars—for both family caregivers and care recipients.

Intersections International
274 Fifth Avenue
New York, NY 10001 USA
212-951-7006
www.intersectionsinternational.org

Intersections International is a New York based non-government organization (NGO) that works at the intersection of communities in conflict. We promote peace through dialogue using direct service programs, advocacy, educational and informational outreach. Founded in 2007, Intersections is a multi-cultural initiative of the Collegiate Churches of New York, the oldest corporation in North America, dating back to 1628.

National Alliance for Caregiving
4720 Montgomery Lane, 2nd Floor
Bethesda, MD 20814
www.caregiving.org/

The not-for-profit National Alliance for Caregiving is a coalition of family caregiving organizations that include grassroots organizations, professional associations, service organizations, disease-specific organizations, a government agency, and corporations.

National Council on the Aging, Inc.
1901 L Street, N.W.
4th Floor
Washington, DC 20036
202-479-1200
www.ncoa.org

The National Council on Aging is a nonprofit service and advocacy organization. Among the caregiving resources accessible on this site is **BenefitsCheckUp®**, a screening tool that directs users to location-specific benefits possibilities.

National Family Caregivers Association
10400 Connecticut Avenue, Suite 500
Kensington, MD 20895–3944
1-800-896-3650
www.nfcacares.org/
E-mail: **info@thefamilycaregiver.org**

The National Family Caregivers Association offers education, support and resources to family caregivers.

National Respite Locator Service
800 Eastowne Drive, Suite 105
Chapel Hill, NC 27514
800-473-1727, ext. 222
www.respitelocator.org/index.html

This Administration on Aging (AOA) site includes a tool that allows users to **get information on state agencies on the aging and available local resources.**

Next Step in Care
E-mail: nextstepincare@uhfnyc.org

The Next Step in Care: Family Caregivers and Health Care Professionals Working Together recognizes, trains, and supports family caregivers who need help during times of transitions in care.

SAGE (Services and Advocacy for GLBT Elders)
305 7th Avenue
15th Floor
New York, NY 10001
212-741-2247
www.sageusa.org

SAGE is the country's largest and oldest organization dedicated to improving the lives of lesbian, gay, bisexual and transgender (LGBT) older adults. Founded in 1978 and headquartered in New York City, SAGE is a national organization that offers supportive services and consumer resources to LGBT older adults and their caregivers, advocates for public policy changes that address the needs of LGBT older people, and provides training for aging providers and LGBT organizations through its **National Resource Center on LGBT Aging**. With offices in New York City, Washington, DC and Chicago, SAGE coordinates a growing network of 21 local **SAGE affiliates** in 15 states and the District of Columbia.

ShareTheCaregiving
National Center for Civic Innovation
121 Avenue of the Americas, 6th Floor
New York, NY 10013
212-991-9688
www.sharethecare.org

This not-for-profit offers education to the caregiving community about the effectiveness of the **Share The Care**™ model. The site provides information on local training seminars, workshops and lectures designed to improve both caregivers' and care recipients' quality of life.

VideoCaregiving
www.videocaregiving.org

Chicago-based Terra Nova Films' Visual Education Center for Family Caregivers offers free online videos providing information on a range of topics like: caregiving and recovery after a stroke; how to approach a discussion about nursing homes; caregiving and Alzheimer's; how to lift and transfer a person who is bedridden and more.

With Compliments of EmblemHealth

www.emblemhealth.com/careforthefamilycaregiver
www.facebook.com/careforthefamilycaregiver

Care for the Family Caregiver

Overview:
EmblemHealth's Care for the Family Caregiver Program

Few jobs are as challenging as being an unpaid family caregiver – no matter how much you love the person in your care. But even if your responsibilities will never be easy, there are certainly ways to make them easier.

CARE FOR THE FAMILY CAREGIVER is an initiative of the Integrative Wellness department that provides information, resources and tools to help manage the challenges and stress of caregiving. Recognizing that family caregivers are the forgotten patients, the program seeks to address some of the needs of unpaid family caregivers, of whom there are some 65.7 million nationwide.

Often called the "silent patients," family caregivers are largely ignored by the health care system, and thus are at risk for depression and illness. With an aging population, medical advances that keep people alive longer, shorter hospital stays, and sophisticated technology that allows sicker people to stay at home, the importance of family caregivers – and the demands on them – will only increase.

EmblemHealth's Web site offers a wealth of information including links about caregiving. To access the Web site go to www.emblemhealth.com, click on "Health & Wellness" at the top menu bar, then go to "Family Caregiver" on the left bar. You'll find numerous links for New York City, regional and national resources.

For more information about EmblemHealth caregiving programs, please contact Gregory Johnson, creator of the Care for the Family Caregiver program, at **gjohnson@emblemhealth.com**.

10 Tips for Family Caregivers

1. Caregiving is a job and respite is your earned right. **Reward yourself** with respite breaks often.

2. **Watch out** for signs of depression, and don't delay in getting professional help when you need it.

3. When people offer help, **accept the offer** and suggest specific things that they can do.

4. **Educate yourself** about your loved one's condition and how to communicate effectively with doctors.

5. There's a difference between caring and doing. **Be open** to technologies and ideas that promote your loved one's independence.

6. **Trust your instincts.** Most of the time they'll lead you in the right direction.

7. Caregivers often do a lot of lifting, pushing, and pulling. **Be good to your back.**

8. Grieve for your losses, and then allow yourself to **dream new dreams.**

9. **Seek support** from other caregivers. There is great strength in knowing you are not alone.

10. **Stand up for your rights** as a caregiver and citizen.

Source: National Family Caregivers Association

Cuidados para el Cuidador de la Familia

Programa Cuidados para el Cuidador de la Familia de EmblemHealth

Pocos trabajos presentan tantos desafíos como el del cuidador de la familia que no recibe ningún pago – no importa cuánto usted quiere a la persona bajo su cuidado. Pero aún cuando sus responsabilidades nunca serán fáciles, hay formas para hacerlas más llavaderas.

CUIDADOS PARA EL CUIDADOR DE LA FAMILIA es una iniciative del deparmentamento de Bienstar Integrado que proporciona información recursos y herramientas para ayudar a manejar los retos y el estrés de la provisión de cuidados. Reconociendo que los cuidadores de la familia son las pacientes olvidados, el programa busca satisfacer algunas de las necesidades de los cuidadores de la familia que no reciben pago, del los cuales hay cerca de 44.5 millones en todo el país.

A menudo llamados los "pacientes silenciosos", los cuidadores de la familia son ignorados en gran medida por el sistema de la atención de la salud y por tanto están a riesgo de depresión y enfermedad. Con un población que envejece, los adelantos médicos que prolongan la vida de las personas, las estancias más cortas en el hospital y la tecnología sofisticada que permite que las personas enfermas se queden en el hogar, la importancia de las cuidadores de la familia – y lo que se espera de ellos – sin duda aumentarán.

El sitio de Internet de EmblemHealth ofrece una gran cantidad de información que incluye enlaces sobre la provisión de cuidados. Para acceso al sitio de Internet, vaya a www.emblemhealth.com, haga clic en "Health & Wellness" en la barra de menú superior, después vaya a "Family Caregiver" en la barra a la izquierda. Encontraré numerosos recursos de la Ciudad de Nueva York, regionales y nacionales.

Para más informacion sobre los programas de provisión de cuidados de EmblemHealth, por favor comuniquese con Gregory Johnson, creador del programa Cuidados para el Cuidador de la Familia, llamanda al : **gjohnson@emblemhealth.com**.

10 Consejos para los Cuidadores de la Familia

1. El ofrecer cuidados es un trabajo y el descanso es el derecho que usted se ha Ganado. **Recompénsese** con períodos de descanso frecuentes.

2. **Esté al tanto** de las señales de depresión y no demore en obtener ayuda professional cuando la necesite.

3. Cuando la gente le ofrezca ayuda, **acepte la oferta** y sugiera cosas específicas que pueden hacer.

4. **Edúquese** sobre la afección de su ser querido y cómo comunicarse eficazmente con los médicos.

5. Hay una diferencia entre cuidar y hacer. **Sea receptivo** a tecnologías e ideas que promueven la independencia de su ser querido.

6. **Confíe en sus instintos.** La mayor parte del tiempo le llevarán por el rumbo correcto.

7. Las personas que proporcionan cuidados a menudo tienen que alzar, empujar y jalar. **Proteja su espalda.**

8. Llore las pérdidas y después permítase **soñar nuevos sueños.**

9. **Busque apoyo** de otros cuidadores. El saber que no está solo le dará una enorme fuerza.

10. **Defienda sus derechos** como cuidador y como ciudadano.

Fuente: National Family Caregivers Association

10 Tips for Family Caregivers

Also available in:
Russian
Chinese
Contact: gjohnson@emblemhealth.com

Helpful Tips for Family Caregivers

FROM: CARE for the FAMILY CAREGIVER; A Place to Start
By: Gregory L. Johnson, EmblemHealth, NYC
Gail Gibson Hunt, National Alliance for Caregiving

Caregiving can require an enormous physical and emotional commitment, as well as some basic skills. The pages that follow provide tips and information on where to start.

CREATE A SAFE ENVIRONMENT AT HOME.

Conduct a home safety inspection of your loved one's home or your own if you are caring for someone there. For example, check for adequate lighting, install grab bars in the bathroom and hook up a cordless phone for emergencies.

Home Safety checklists are available on the Internet and from the AARP. (Go to www.aarp.org, and search Home Safety Caregiving Checklist.)

GET CAREGIVER TRAINING.

See out educational resources in caregiving. (See Caregiver Training section that follows.) For example, learn the correct way to transfer a loved one from a bed to a wheelchair. This can help you avoid serious injury to yourself and the person for whom you are caring.

In addition, learn how to properly bathe someone with mobility problems. This can reduce the risk of hospitalization for chronic sores and infections.

MAINTAIN MEDICAL RECORDS.

Keep a current, complete list of all medications and physicians, along with notes on medical history. Be sure to take this if you accompany your loved one to doctor's visits.

Most care recipients (93%) take at least one prescription drug. It's important to keep a list of all medications the care recipient is currently taking. Be sure to also record the dosage or strength, such as 10mg; for what condition the drug is taken; and how often it is taken, such as twice a day. A drug regimen may change often, so be sure to make regular updates. Pharmacists in particular are valuable resources for medication information.

If your loved one has access to a personal health record (PHR), use it to record symptoms, doctor visits, medications and other important health information.

LEARN ABOUT THE DISEASE.

Find out all you can about the disease the care recipient has, its treatments and the prognosis. Armed with this information, you and your family will have a better idea what to expect in the future and how you can help. This information can help you with planning.

LEARN HOW TO COMMUNICATE WITH HEALTHCARE PROFESSIONALS.

In order to be a better advocate for your loved one, understand and use the terminology that doctors, nurses, discharge planners, therapists and other health care professionals use in discussing the case. Be calm but firm in advocating for being a part of the health care support service decision-making team.

Minimize stress, especially during holidays.

Holidays can be especially stressful for both caregivers and care recipients. Try to reduce stress, simplify activities, relax, slow the pace and ensure that there is plenty of quiet time to reminisce.

Get the extended family involved in caregiving.

Organize and hold a family meeting involving all decision makers. Identify and discuss the issues of providing care for the family member in need.

Ask for help with household activities.

Seek help with yard work and other household tasks. Consider asking a friend or neighbor for help. Hire someone to mow the lawn. Look into delivery services for groceries or drugstore items.

Delegate to friends and family.

Remember, be specific when asking for help from family and friends: "Can Jill come for a couple of hours on Saturdays to stay with Grandma while I do the shopping?" or "Can George mow the lawn every other week now that Dad can't do it any longer?

Manage your time

Keep an appointment book or calendar to schedule your daily activities, including doctor's visits. Some computer programs or personal devices can help you schedule and manage your time. Consider using an online calendar you can share with other family members on the Internet, such as Google Calendar.

Seek help that meets your situation.

Each caregiving situation is unique. For example, if you care for someone who is not living with you and lives a long distance away, you may face special logistical, financial and emotional challenges. Seek out resources that meet your special long distance needs; for example, consider using a geriatric care manager.

Caregiver Health: Taking Care of Yourself

Caregivers face multiple responsibilities and complex demands of their time, energy and efforts. Many caregivers work full-time outside the home and care for spouses and children as well as frail or ill family members. As a result, caregivers can take a significant physical and psychological toll. It is therefore important for you as a caregiver to take steps to maintain your health and well-being.

While many caregivers report feeling loved, appreciated and needed as a result of their caregiving, many feel worried, frustrated, sad or depressed and overwhelmed. It is important to build a support system and seek help so you can take care of yourself as well.

Take breaks from caregiving.

Find ways to take breaks from caregiving. Studies have shown that caregiving for prolonged periods of time can adversely affect both your physical and psychological health. It can also negatively affect your employment status and ability to earn a living. Many caregivers report that it is difficult to balance the needs of caring for older parents and other family members with meeting their own personal needs. Seek out respite care to give yourself a break.

Take breaks as often as you can. Take time everyday to engage in a relaxing activity. Read a book, rest, take a walk or exercise, meditate or pray. Just be sure to schedule time for yourself away from your caregiving obligations. While it may seem selfish, taking regular breaks will help you "recharge" and be a better caregiver.

Take steps to safeguard your own health and well-being.

It is important that you attend to your own health. Do not neglect your own health needs at the expense of caring for someone else.

As a caregiver, you should make the following part of your routine:

- Go to your primary care physician for regular check-ups, mammograms and prostate exams.

- Get a flu shot and pneumonia vaccine. Supplies of the flu vaccine often run short, so be sure to obtain one early in the flu season, including vaccinations against seasonal influenza and new strains, such as H1N1. Late fall and early winter are ideal. Ask your health care provider about which vaccines are right for you.

- Take medications and monitor your own health with the diligence and attention you give to those you care for.

- Be sure to take time for regular exercise. Even a short walk daily can help you maintain your physical condition, reduce your risk for certain diseases and provide psychological benefit.

- Eat a sensible, healthy diet that includes fruits and vegetables.

- Consider taking classes and engaging in stress-reduction and coping techniques. Some find yoga, meditation and other relaxation techniques particularly helpful.

- Continue to participate in religious or spiritual activities, as well as recreational activities, sports, hobbies or simply spending time with friends.

CONSIDER JOINING A SUPPORT GROUP.

Many caregivers report that isolation is their number one source of stress. Look for a local support group for caregivers, where you will be able to share feelings of isolation and frustration. Check the resources in this book and the Internet for "self-help" and support groups. For example, a local chapter of the Alzheimer's Association (see www.alz.org) might hold regular support group meetings for those who care for people with Alzheimer's.

Many people find solace in sharing feelings and seeking emotional support from others who understand first-hand the challenges of caregiving. If it is difficult to get out to a support group meeting, you might find it helpful to connect with others on Internet-based Discussion Boards. Many caregiving Web sites listed in this handbook include such online communities for family caregivers.

About the Authors

REVEREND GREGORY L. JOHNSON is an ordained Inter-faith Minister serving at The Marble Collegiate Church in New York City. In both his professional and private life, he has been a tireless champion for increased awareness, understanding and support for family caregiving. This includes serving as:

- Director of Community Outreach and the Creator of the Care for the Family Caregiver program at Emblem Health, a New York-based health care corporation.
- A Member of the US Department of Health and Human Services' National Family Caregiver Support Program Review Task Force.
- FELLOW: NYAM (New York City Academy of Medicine)
- Co-founder of: NYCFCC (New York City Family Caregiver Coalition—2003); NYCP4FC Corps (New York City Partnership for Family Caregiving Corps—2012).
- Co-author of the booklet, Care for the Family Caregiver; A Place to Start, written for the 2005 White House Conference on Aging.
- Caregiver to his partner of 41 years, Joseph Polacek, who passed in May 2011.

- Long distance family caregiver for I. Wayan Suardika (Putra) their adopted son in Bali who died in 2005 at the age of 40.

Reverend Johnson has received numerous awards, honors and recognitions within the fields of health care, family caregiving and service to others. He is also a member of Speaker Christine Quinn's NYC Council's Hate Crimes Task Force for Clergy.

Through family caregiving, he is committed to helping others *celebrate the things we share in common and honor those that make us unique: living the Golden Rule.* Reverend Johnson resides in New York City and Bali, Indonesia.

REVEREND MARION A. GAMBARDELLA has helped others achieve wholeness through the integration of mind, body and spirit for more than two decades. She obtained her teaching, counseling and licensing credentials through The Unity Institute and The Association of Unity Churches and also through Religious Science International (Science of Mind).

Marion—Co-Chair of the New York City Partnership for Family Caregiver Corps.—was ordained as an Interfaith Minister through The New Seminary of New York. In addition, she has served as:

- Minister of the Unity Center of Flushing, New York, and Unity Center of Monterey, California.
- Director of The Unity Energy Healing and Holistic Center in Sacramento, California.

- Associate Minister and the Director of The Health and Wellness Ministry and Community Outreach Programs at The Unity Center of New York
- Caregiver for her husband, Giovanni Consiglio, who made his transition on February 21, 2012, after a four year illness.

She has been a frequent speaker at the Unity Center of New York Sunday Services at the Lincoln Center and a guest speaker/workshop leader at various Church, Holistic and Spiritual Centers Coast to Coast and has appeared on numerous health and wellness programs on National Television. Rev. Marion has received various awards for her outreach community work including one from the U.S. House of Representatives-Certificate of Special Congressional Recognition for her outstanding and invaluable service to the Community. Marion provides one-on-one spiritual counseling and conducts monthly Caregiving Support Group Meetings in New York City where she resides.

About the Editor

LISA ISOM is a mother, wife, daughter, sister—and former family caregiver. An award-winning journalist, editor and author of several books, Lisa has written extensively on health and wellness, business, law, health care reform—and family caregiving.

Her byline has appeared in a number of professional business management journals, as well as national news publications, ranging from The New York Observer to Essence magazine.

About the Creative Director

C. LINDA DINGLER has had over 40 years of experience working in the publishing industry. She has been a book designer all of her career, and has worked with such illustrious authors as Hillary Clinton, Dr. Mehmet Oz and President Jimmy Carter.

About the Cover Illustrator

SASHA KINENS is an artist who paints narratives, at turns allegorical and visceral, ethereal and lingering. Another world created by intricate sets, costumes and wigs. Her art is informed by classical realism, inspired by the pre-Raphaelites and Symbolists of the nineteenth century. She consistently weaves a twenty-first century outlook into the fabric of each work.

CPSIA information can be obtained at www.ICGtesting.com
Printed in the USA
BVOW03s1350260314

348849BV00001B/1/P